First published 1995 A&C Black (Publishers) Limited
35 Bedford Row, London WC1R 4JH

ISBN 0-7136-4125-8
A CIP catalogue record for this book is available
from the British Library.

Acknowledgements

Photographs by Zul Mukhida.

Design by Helen White.
Cover design by Jane Tassie.

Photographic and design direction by Karen
Bryant-Mole.

The author and publisher would like to thank all
the children who appear in the photographs.

They also wish to thank the Early Learning Centre,
Swindon for providing the equipment featured on
pages 2 and 3.

Printed and bound by Partenaires Fabrication,
Malesherbes, France.

Is it heavy?

Karen Bryant-Mole

A&C Black • London

short

Leila has used a few blocks to make
this **short** tower.

tall

Leila is using lots of blocks to make
a **tall** tower.

taller

Lou's sister is **taller** than Lou.

tallest

Lou's mum is taller than Lou and his sister.
Lou's mum is the **tallest**.

long

Alex is lying on her **long** bed.
There is plenty of room to stretch out.

short

Her doll's bed is **short**.
Could Alex lie in it?

shorter

Sam has some vegetables.
The courgette is **shorter** than the leek.

shortest

But the carrot is the **shortest** of them all.

large

An elephant is a **large** animal.
You can sit on an elephant.

small

A guinea pig is **small**.
You can hold one in your arms.

thin

Charlie is eating a **thin** sandwich.

thick

Leila has a **thick** sandwich.
Her sandwich is quite hard to hold!

wide

Holly opens the **wide** gate
to let the tractor drive out.

narrow

Emma and Leila open the **narrow** gate
and squeeze through.

full

Lou's glass is **full** of milk.

empty

Lou has drunk the milk.
His glass is **empty**.

deep

In the **deep** swimming pool, the water
comes right up to Sarah's chin.

shallow

In the **shallow** paddling pool, the water only comes up to her ankles.

heavy

Charlie's box is full of toys.
It is too **heavy** for him to carry.

light

Sam's box of sweets is easy to carry.
It is very **light**.

balance

Emma sits on one end of the see-saw.
Leila sits on the other end.

Both ends are off the ground.
The see-saw is **balanced**.

Index

This index will help you find the Buzzwords in this book.

balance	22-23
deep	18
empty	17
full	16
heavy	20
large	10
light	21
long	6
narrow	15
shallow	19
short	2, 7
shorter	8
shortest	9
small	11
tall	3
taller	4
tallest	5
thick	13
thin	12
wide	14

Things to do

People pictures

You will need a roll of old wallpaper. Roll out a length of wallpaper, with the plain side towards you. Lie down on the paper and ask a friend to draw round you. Now paint or crayon the outline to look just like you. Cut out your picture and put it on a wall or door. Help your friends to make pictures of themselves, too, and then compare pictures to find out who is the tallest.

Jigsaw puzzles

Find two old Christmas or birthday cards. Cut one card into four large pieces. Cut the other into lots of small pieces. Now try to put the shapes back together, so that you can see the pictures again. Which is easier, the puzzle with a few large shapes or the puzzle with lots of small shapes?

Guessing game

Find two boxes that are exactly the same. Ice-cream tubs would be just right. Fill one box with something light, like cotton wool, and the other with something heavy, like stones. Ask a friend to look at the boxes and guess which is heavier. You friend may think that they both weigh the same. Now let your friend pick up the boxes. Which feels heavier? Try playing this game with lots of different sorts of objects.

How to use this book

Children's understanding of concepts is fundamentally linked to their ability to comprehend and use relevant language. This book is designed to help children understand the vocabulary associated with measurement.

Measurement is an important area within mathematics. Before children can begin to measure using standard units they need to understand that objects have sizes and quantities. This book helps children to develop that understanding by explaining key words connected with measurement and by encouraging children to use these words in everyday situations.

Most of the pairs of words featured on each double page are opposites, such as **full** and **empty.** Other pairs of words, such as **taller** and **tallest**, are comparative. Children can be encouraged to think about the words and to discuss whether or not they are opposites.

Each word in this book is explained through a colour photograph, which illustrates it, and a phrase, which uses that word in context. As well as explaining words that are basic to the understanding of measurement, the book can be used in a number of other ways.

Children can think of objects, other than the one in the photograph, that can be described using a particular Buzzword. The Buzzword **wide** does not just describe gates. It can be applied to many other objects. Roads, ribbons, paths, leaves and rivers, can all be described as **wide**.

Objects can often be described using more than one measuring word. This book can help a child give as full a description as possible. A chest of drawers might be described using the Buzzwords **heavy**, **large**, **wide** and **full**.

Some of the pages introduce the children to the concept of comparison. This concept can be applied to almost all the Buzzwords in the book. As well, as describing a sandwich as either **thick** or **thin**, it could be compared with other sandwiches and described as **thicker** or **thinner**.

Once children have understood the concept of comparing two objects they can begin to arrange three or more objects in order. A group of children might draw around their feet and, by comparison, order the length from the **shortest** to the **longest.**